Contents

Winter   6

Spring   10

Summer   15

Autumn   21

Winter again   24

Things to do   28

Seasons words and index   30

Look for leaf buds on winter branches.

← an ash twig

Winter

Winter! Shivery winter . . .
The path's like a skating rink.
It's dark before bedtime and
cold as penguins' feet!

Cold, clear nights are the best nights for seeing the stars.

Penguins live in the Antarctic where it is always icy cold.

Seasons Turning

Mick Manning
and Brita Granström

W
FRANKLIN WATTS
LONDON·SYDNEY

For Haworth Primary School,
West Yorkshire

First published in 2001
by Franklin Watts,
96 Leonard Street,
London EC2A 4XD

Franklin Watts Australia
56 O'Riordan Street
Alexandria
NSW 2015

The illustrations in this book have been drawn
by both Mick and Brita

Text and illustrations © 2001 Mick Manning
and Brita Granström
Series editor: Rachel Cooke
Art director: Jonathan Hair

Printed in Hong Kong, China
A CIP catalogue record is available from
the British Library.
Dewey Classification 574.5
ISBN 0 7496 4182 7

Evergreen plants like holly and ivy don't lose their leaves in the winter.

holly

People used to think that holly and ivy were magical because they were always green.

ivy

Birds like to eat...

...mealtime leftovers like cheese, bread and bacon rind.

But the
seasons
are turning.
Drip, drip, drip!
Winter's slowly thawing . . .

sunflower seed

It's good to feed the birds
in winter. They need
water in icy weather, too.

peanuts

grain

←new green shoots

new green leaves→

Spring

. . . Thawing into spring.
Noisy spring! Bees buzz.
Birds sing. Spring rain
drums on the roof.
The days grow longer . . .

In spring,
thrushes sing
to attract a mate.

Grebes grow bright
new feathers . . .

. . . to replace their
dull winter colours.

Stoats lose their thick winter fur.

catkins →

← pussy willow

11

swallow

Some birds migrate – they spend the winter in warmer places and return in the spring.

Spring is blossoming!
Fresh leaves grow.
Birds build nests.
The weather is warmer.
The seasons are turning . . .

A bird has nested in an old teapot!

Bumble bees build nests in spring.

Newts lay their eggs underwater on pond weed.

13

redshank chicks

Summer finds:

a snail

a ladybird

a tiger moth

14

Baby birds follow their mums.

Summer

. . . Blooming into summer.
Take a deep breath and
smell summer!

New butterflies come out.

Butterflies lay eggs on leaves.

They hatch into caterpillars.

The caterpillars pupate.

15

Summer sun! Summer
holidays by the sea!
Sun creams. Ice creams.
Sizzling barbecues and days
that just go on and on . . .

Holiday finds:

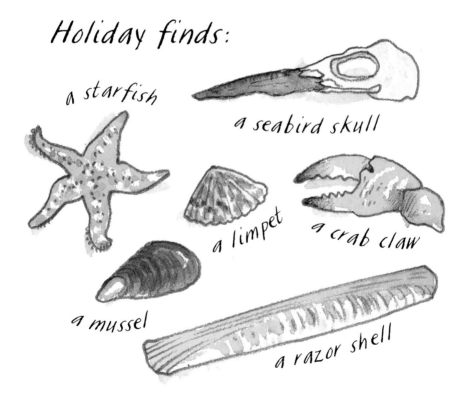

a starfish

a seabird skull

a limpet

a crab claw

a mussel

a razor shell

a gull feather

a lolly stick

a spider

an ear of wheat

an ear of barley

18

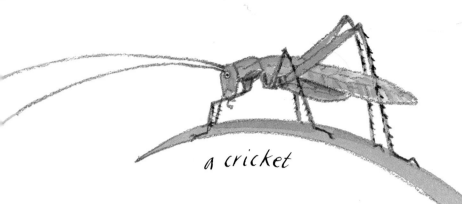
a cricket

Then one day, the holidays are over. The wheat is cut. Summer's nearly gone. The seasons are turning again . . .

Wheat fields are home to lots of wildlife – from insects to harvest mice.

a harvestman

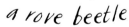
a rove beetle

a ladybird

a grasshopper

a harvest mouse

Autumn is the time when the fields are ploughed.

Autumn gales help to blow down dead leaves. The leaves slowly rot to make rich soil for new plant life.

20

Earthworms love to eat dead leaves.

Autumn

. . . Turning into autumn.
Crisp and cool autumn!
Dead leaves crunch underfoot.
Gaggles of wild geese fly
honking overhead.

Some birds from cold places, like these wild geese, migrate in the autumn to places with warmer winters.

21

Autumn winds shake the trees.
The days grow shorter.
Everywhere, nature smells
damp and mushroomy.
The seasons are turning
full circle . . .

a parasol

a chanterelle

Wild fungi can look
pretty but can be
poisonous!

a puffball

a dead leaf

a sycamore seed

an acorn

blackberries

rowan berries

a conker

a pine cone

Winter again

Winter's back. The path's like a skating rink again.

Some animals sleep through the cold winter weather. Their long sleep is called hibernation.

Dormice sleep in grass nests.

Bears sleep in a den underground.

Stoats grow thick winter fur and some turn white.

Butterflies crawl into nooks and crannies to hibernate.

25

It's dark before bedtime -
and cold as
penguins' feet . . .

The seasons are
a cycle – each one
linked to the
one before and
the one after.

Even in the middle of winter,
spring buds are already growing.

← a horse chestnut twig with
sticky buds.

27

Things to do

Why not keep a notebook
of the seasons?
Try these seasonal
activities, too.

Winter
Feed the birds and give them
water (see page 8). In snowy weather,
make a snowball lantern. Pile
up snowballs into a
cone shape and pop
a nightlight inside.

Spring
Hang up a bird box
for nesters like tits and
sparrows. An old watering
can in a shady spot makes
a good nest for robins,
flycatchers or wagtails.

Summer

Make a minibeast hotel for slugs, snails and woodlice. Hollow out half a melon or large grapefruit and cut a door in to it. Your guests get bed and breakfast.

Autumn

Collect pretty autumn leaves and press them between sheets of tissue or blotting paper. Put a heavy book on top and leave to dry in a warm place.

Seasons words and index

Antarctic - the area that surrounds the most southerly point on Earth. The Antarctic has seasons but it is always very cold. Page 6

autumn - the season after summer and before winter when it begins to cool down. Pages 20-24, 26

buds - the points on a plant from where new leaves, shoots or flowers grow. Pages 6, 27

evergreen - plants that keep their leaves all year round. Page 7

fungi - a group of living things which includes mushrooms and toadstools. Page 22

hibernation - the long sleep some animals take to survive the cold winter. Pages 24, 25

migrate - to move with the seasons to find food. Birds migrate from cooler to warmer places for the winter and back again for the summer. Pages 12, 21

pupate - to change from a caterpillar to a pupa, the third part of a butterfly's lifecycle. Page 15

spring - the season between winter and summer when it begins to get warmer. Pages 10-13, 26, 27

summer - the hottest season of the year. Pages 14-19, 26

thawing - melting. Ice thaws into water. Pages 9, 10

winter - the coldest season of the year. Pages 6-9, 11, 12, 24-27